A Littl

Old Roses

Hazel Le Rougetel

Illustrated by
ROSEANNE SANDERS

Appletree Press

First published in 1992 by
The Appletree Press Ltd,
7 James Street South, Belfast BT2 8DL
Copyright © 1992 The Appletree Press Ltd.
Printed in the E.C. All rights reserved.

A Little Book of Old Roses

A catalogue record for this book is available in
The British Library.

ISBN: 0-86281-333-6

9 8 7 6 5 4 3 2 1

Introduction

The last half of the twentieth century has witnessed a surge of interest in the older roses, largely due to stimulation by English rose grower Graham Thomas through his books and practical demonstration. For the National Trust he planned the extensive Rose Garden within mellowed walls at Mottisfont, near Stockbridge, in Hampshire, where rose history may be traced from his beautiful presentation.

Heritage rose societies flourish in America, Australia, and New Zealand; over four hundred enthusiasts attended an international conference in Christchurch in 1990. The Royal National Rose Society has recently formed an Historic Roses Group to emphasize its concern for all classes, which are well represented in its Gardens of the Rose near St. Albans, Hertfordshire. In North America there is a comprehensive collection at the Morton Arboretum, Lisle, Illinois, and another, very attractively displayed, can be seen in the Cranford Memorial Rose Garden, Brooklyn Botanic Garden, New York.

This little book aims to tell the story of rose development from medieval times to the beginning of this century, with emphasis on those varieties cherished by mankind. The twenty-eight old roses illustrated have been chosen as examples of the main classes and these are augmented by mention of over one hundred more in the text – almost all available today. Guidance is given on how best to grow them informally as flowering shrubs of diverse form, and suggestions are made for suitable plants to use as complementary companions.

Rosa eglanteria

This European species has long been used in gardens, as shown at the Roman villa in Fishbourne, near Chichester, where it brightens surrounding evergreen planting. In medieval and Tudor times it embellished arbours and was one of the first roses to be taken abroad by colonists and often used as windbreak hedges in bleak country. William Penn's initial instructions to use "what grows quickest" included the sweet briar, President Jefferson planted many in his Virginian garden and landscaper "Capability" Brown included them for wilderness planting at Petworth, Sussex in the eighteenth century.

The sweet briar spans 12 x 8 ft / 3.5 x 2.5 m and clear pink blooms are followed by shiny orange-red fruit; the fragrant fine foliage, its greatest asset, is intensified by rain and also by clipping. It will tolerate any condition, though perhaps looks best in grass or on woodland perimeter with *RR. canina, arvensis, villosa* and shorter *pimpinellifolia* to the fore – other European species and appropriate companions for Shakespeare's "Eglantine".

Early hybrids included two doubles of compact habit; Scarlet Sweet Briar is eye-catching with little scent, whereas pink-tinted Manning's Blush has more and a later introduction, Janet's Pride is semi-double with blush markings on bright pink flowers. A century ago, Lord Penzance bred a number of large, lax varieties only suitable for bigger gardens, one of the most attractive being Lady Penzance which is tinted yellow, salmon and copper.

The Apothecary's Rose

Long before "roses red and white" were recorded in early descriptions of gardens, this Gallica had been appreciated for its usefulness. By the thirteenth century it was grown extensively around Provins near Paris, its scent-retaining petals used for a famed conserve and medicaments – *officinalis* denotes a plant approved by the apothecaries. In 1652, the English herbalist Nicholas Culpeper prescribed a "decoction of Red Roses" for pains in the head, eyes, throat, gums, head and stomach, while John Winthrop, first Governor of Massachusetts advised his family, about to join him from England, to bring the conserve with them and a friend sent roses pink, red and white, to grow in his Boston garden.

Gallicas are the tidiest of old summer-flowering roses and suitable for small gardens with compact bushes, having rather rigid, rough-textured dark green leaves and bristly stems. Wonderfully-fragrant flowers – always poised on stiff stalks and ranging from palest blush through every shade of pink to deep maroon – provide a galaxy of beauty over six weeks at midsummer.

The Apothecary's Rose was correctly grown with other herbs and the same association can well be maintained today; small blue flowers of some herbs complementing the deep tones of Gallicas. Hyssop, sage or rue can be planted with darkest Tuscany (also known as Old Velvet) and deep magenta Conditorum, backed by rosemary with purple Cardinal de Richelieu and blush Duchesse de Montebello.

Rosa Mundi

In 1846 a leading American rose grower, William Prince of Flushing, New York, listed 93 "striped, variegated, mottle or marbled" Gallicas. Comparatively few endured, unlike the earliest: Rosa Mundi. No agreement has been reached on how this name arose or on its first appearance, but Sir Thomas Hanmer stated, "first found in Norfolke a few years since, upon a branch of the common Red Rose and from thence multiplied" (*The Garden Book*, 1659). Like the Apothecary's Rose in every respect, except that the light crimson petals are striped with blush, this lovely rose has maintained a place in gardens ever since.

However, the majority of variegated Gallicas are double, their closely-packed petals arranged differently. Petals, for example, reflexed with defined deep-crimson markings in Tricolor de Flandre and rolling pale lilac towards a crimson centre for Président de Sèze. Camaieux has a rather looser assembly, incurling with crimson and purple fading to magenta and lilac, and an abundance of petals in Charles de Mills, seemingly shorn flat, are flushed with every deep, sumptuous shade.

A careful choice of companion is necessary for these charmers: a short flowering time warrants no distraction. Back them with shrubs of sober foliage – a viburnum or hardy hebe to flower before or after the roses – and underplant with discreet *Ajuga repens*, *Viola labradorica* or *Geranium sanguineum striatum*.

Céleste

If space dictated choice of one old summer-flowering rose to represent Albas (the tallest group, once known as "tree roses"), Céleste could well display their particular qualities. Making a good bush of some 6 x 4 ft / 1.8 x 1.2 m with new green wood, few prickles and beautiful soft grey-green foliage, it provides perfect foil for delicate pink blooms of pure fragrance. Semi-double, they unfurl gracefully from a perfectly scrolled bud to become slightly deeper in the centre around a small group of golden stamens. Céleste, like all Albas, is comparatively disease-free and tolerates harsh conditions.

The earliest of the group, *R. a semi-plena*, the old white rose grown with the red Apothecary's in medieval times, was taken by the House of York as its emblem, as was the other by the Lancastrians. It was also used in medicine, particularly for treating eyes, and in the perfume industry. *R.a. maxima*, known as Great Double White and also the Jacobite Rose on account of association with Bonnie Prince Charlie, has many petals of full blooms in darker glaucous foliage. The aptly named Great Maiden's Blush, with reflexing petals paling at the perimeter and of beguiling scent, has been a firm favourite over many years.

Old Albas are well displayed as stalwart shrubs in a broad border at Castle Howard, near York, where phlox of soft shades infil after midsummer and glaucous hosta foliage blends below.

Königin von Dänemarck

New Albas were developed in the early nineteenth century, mostly fully double and of great charm, Queen of Denmark proving perhaps to be the best seducer. Victorian rosarian, Thomas Rivers, records "so much was this esteemed when first raised from seed that plants from Germany cost five guineas each in England". Deep pink on opening, reflexed blooms become softer around a button eye and are well displayed against dark glaucous foliage. An indisputable recommendation must be its choice by Graham Thomas for his midsummer buttonhole.

Twenty-one Albas were listed in the 1845 catalogue of Hovery's Cambridge Nurseries, Boston, and include "superb Queen of Denmark" and "exquisite Félicité Parmentier". Of the two, the latter makes a slightly-smaller bush with unusual features: foliage is light green and buds have a yellow tint. This is lost when it opens to pale pink petals deepening inwards and fading to cream at the edges of a somewhat globular bloom. Madame Legras de St. Germain, more vigorous, is pristine white with unique yellow shading in the centre of a very full flower. Later on, a smaller Alba, Pompon Blanc Parfait was introduced. With dainty pale pink flowers fading to almost white and typical Alba foliage of appropriate scale on a 4 ft / 1.2 m bush, this is well suited to limited space. With all these roses, simple flowers such as campanula, foxglove, aquilegia, saponaria and dianthus complete a satisfying picture.

Kazanlik

Accounts of sweetly-scented Damask roses date back to long ago in countries of the Eastern Mediterranean, although no English records appear until the sixteenth century and they were probably taken to western America by early Spanish missionaries. A natural variation, or sport, from *R. damascena*, York and Lancaster, with irregular pink and white blotches was believed to signify union of the 2 royal Houses. Kazanlik, a summer-flowerer, gets its name from a district in Bulgaria, also known as the Valley of the Roses, stretching some 60 miles, where this rose has been grown extensively since the beginning of the eighteenth century for the attar of roses industry.

Quatre Saisons or Autumn Damask (*R. damascena semperflorens*) is unique among old garden roses in flowering from June to October and even earlier blooms of so-called "monthly roses" were forced against heated walls at Chelsea Physic Garden in the eighteenth century.

These early Damasks have loose, semi-double flowers, white or light pink (called *R. pallida* by the apothecaries) and slender hips compared with rotund and oval of Gallicas and Albas. Their foliage also differs. Round, soft, pale-green leaves on bristly stems form somewhat spindly, lax bushes, less desirable as garden roses than later hybrids. They are best grown naturally in a wild setting, placed behind a shrub on which they may tumble near a seat or path, where their alluring scent may be savoured.

Madame Hardy

As with the Albas, there was a spate of new Damasks at the beginning of the nineteenth century. One raised from seed by the Superintendent of the Luxembourg Gardens, Paris, in 1832, was named Madame Hardy for his wife. At the time, Thomas Rivers of the Sawbridgeworth Nursery thought a more magnificent rose did not exist, and early praise also came from America and Canada for the full-petalled white roses with a green eye. Twentieth-century writers continue to commend it ecstatically. The large bush of 5 x 5 ft / 1.5 x 1.5 m is lax and sometimes needs support.

Isapahan, slightly smaller, produces clear pink blooms in clusters on an upright bush, although Marie Louise, of the same size, is inclined to hang unusual purplish-pink heavy-headed flowers. This lovely Damask was produced at Malmaison, the Empress Josephine's famous rose garden. Leda, or Painted Damask, so called because carmine buds tip the white petals of a rounded flower, is unusually compact (3 x 3 ft / 90 x 90 cm) and William Prince forecast in 1846 that it would be a favourite for some time. It is well shown, tidily bordering a lawn, at Mottisfont today.

These summer-flowering Damasks of various habit are well suited to mixed-border planting. To make the most of their flowering time, do not plant any distracting "hot" colours near their paler shades. One, perhaps Marie Louise, could well be grown against a wall near a window or patio for maximum enjoyment of midsummer scent.

Rosa x centifolia

This historic rose had long been recorded before it was developed further in Holland during the seventeenth century when it often appeared in Flemish flower paintings – one of its names is Rose des Peintres. In England, Centifolias have long been cherished: they were the best-selling roses of nurseries in the mid-eighteenth century, fashionable Regency ladies liked to adorn their hair with a "full blown Provence Rose" (not to be confused with Provins, relating to Gallicas) and William Paul, eminent Victorian rosarian, considered this class to produce some of the finest globular-shaped roses grown. The somewhat unflattering name of cabbage roses came about on account of their petals overlapping in that form when half open.

Two early nineteenth-century variations have unique characteristics: *R. c. bullata*, with extraordinary puckered foliage, bronze when young, is known as the Lettuce-leaved Rose, while *R. c. cristata* has the popular name of Chapeau de Napoléon, on account of the tricorne-shaped winged calyx. The lovely late flowerer, Unique Blanche, discovered in Suffolk in 1757, has almost transparent petals of fine, silky texture, and is mentioned in accounts of early colonial gardens.

Coarse, limp foliage and stout, well-armed stems make *Centifolia* bushes somewhat ungainly, but charm is maintained by strongly-fragrant, voluptuous flowers inclining their heads appealingly to billowing plants such as *Alchemilla mollis* in order to hide the lower supports.

Rose de Meaux

Some neater Centifolias are useful for growing in containers or for fronting a border, the smallest being clear pink de Meaux which has miniature flowers and foliage (2 x 2 ft / 60 x 60 cm). It was known before most of the hybrid Centifolias and also blooms earlier than they do (Rivers judged it "desirable for its spring-gladdening flowers") and it remained popular for a long time. Ombrée Parfait is slightly larger and provides a good contrast with its purple tones, its lax form fitting a wide tub. Petite d'Hollande may reach 4 ft / 1.2 m but has excellent discipline, holding small typical Centifolia-pink flowers erect in groups, which last well on a compact bush, thus making it suitable for a large terracotta pot. This trio will provide flowers for more than two months provided four points are borne in mind: the container must be of adequate depth, drainage efficient, and the planting medium should be "open". Roses hate to have compacted roots, as happen with frequent watering and this is the fourth essential proviso, especially necessary in hot climates. A good planting mixture consists of $1/2$ potting compost, $1/4$ each of fibre and grit, plus a handful of charcoal (remains of a wood fire or bonfire are useful) and to replace the top 2–3 inches in spring.

Any of the smaller old roses, provided they are neat growers, are suitable for pots on a tiny garden patio where their scent may be enjoyed. When flowering is over, they can be replaced with container-grown plants of, for example, tender late-flowering fuchsias.

Common Moss

This rose first occurred as a Centifolia sport in Europe before the end of the seventeenth century. Philip Miller brought one back to Chelsea Physic Garden from Leiden in 1727 to wide acclaim, and mosses remained in demand when most old roses fell from favour during Victorian times. Robert Buist exhibited 20 varieties at the Pennsylvania Horticultural Society Show in June 1855. However, the Common Moss has always held its own, with fragrant pink flowers offset by soft, fresh, green-mossed flower stalks and buds, a unique feature due to enlarged glands, scented and sticky, varying from dark reddish brown to pale lime green in subsequent introductions.

These vary in colour and size from tiny, light crimson Little Gem and creamy pink Mousseline, both 3 ft / 90 cm, to lofty William Lobb, 8 ft / 2.5 m or more if supported, which displays purple-lavender blooms to advantage. Henri Martin presents deep crimson flowers in abundance on an open 6 ft / 1.8 m bush, while Nuits de Young is shorter, with slender form, small maroon flowers and bronze-tinted foliage.

Mosses, and indeed all the old roses, should not be pruned h rd like modern varieties. Aim to maintain well-formed shrubs by removing all spindly growth and cutting out old wood from the base at the end of July to encourage new long shoots. These may be shortened by $^1/_3$ in February to present a balanced bush. However, Gallicas and Albas need less attention in this respect.

Double White (Scots Briar)

A small hardy species, *R. pimpinellifolia*, flourishing on windswept shore or limestone heath, was used to develop many varieties by the two brothers Brown at a nursery near Perth in the early nineteenth century. Over 200 varieties were offered originally but, with the advent of long-flowering roses, their popularity declined and today's list is small. However, their hardiness in any situation deserves recognition, and a good choice is provided in the Gardens of the Rose when they flower in early summer.

One of the best, Double White, has small cupped blooms of fresh fragrance and, when planted with semi-double pink Andrewsii and single purple Mrs Colville, will produce a beautiful hedge. As these roses spread freely by suckering, density is assured, and they may be freely trimmed with shears in winter. A topiary bush of one of the marbled pink-and-blush varieties will make a spectacular mound of colour in June. Around 1830, hybrids were introduced in America and England: Harison's Yellow and Williams's Yellow, distinguished by stamens or a central green eye and have bright semi-double flowers.

Scots Briars look well planted on a wild bank with heather and cistus flourish in dry, sandy soil to provide continuous interest. They are among the first roses of summer, poised in delicate ferny foliage, followed by leaves of autumnal tints and unusual darkest maroon hips like large blackcurrants.

Stanwell Perpetual

Within a decade of the introduction of this rose in 1839 by Lee of Hammersmith, rose growers were extolling its virtues. An assessment by Thomas Rivers – "one of the sweetest and prettiest of autumnal roses" was repeated by William Prince. The long-flowering period of "large double pale blush flowers of exquisite fragrance" was emphasised by Robert Buist, and, a century on, Edward Bunyard felt it should be in every garden, as it was rarely without flowers from May to December.

From its parents, the Autumn Damask and *R. pimpinellifolia*, Stanwell Perpetual gained valuable qualities. It is tolerant of adverse weather conditions, be they drought or frost. Out-growing pliant stems and a naturally lax habit result in a graceful bush requiring space – ideal for a wild area of the garden. However, it may be controlled in a border by attaching the stems to a low perimeter wire firmly pegged to the ground, some cutting out old wood and tieing down new shoots in August is necessary to keep the whole to $2^1/_2$ ft / 75 cm, half the normal height. Good gloves are essential for manipulating well-armed stems.

Any account of this rose should include mention of the purple mottling sometimes evident on older foliage. This is innate, not a disease, and does not detract from the overall appeal of this chance seedling from Stanwell – a rose likely to remain popular throughout the world for many years to come.

Portland Rose

This rose looks somewhat similar to *R. gallica* from which it may have been descended. Distinction lies in deeper colour and, importantly, a longer flowering habit inherited from the Autumn Damask, Scarlet Four Seasons. It was known in Italy before the end of the eighteenth century and obtained by the Duchess of Portland, an enthusiastic, knowledgeable gardener who exchanged roses with the French Empress Josephine at a time when general trading between the two countries was suspended by war, and it is believed that the French royal gardener, Dupont, named this one for her.

In turn, the Portland Rose gave rise to the development of Rose du Roi, to be known in England as Lee's Perpetual Crimson. With very fragrant large semi-double flowers, it has compact form, and the Rose du Roi à Fleur Pourpre varies only in deeper shadings. Robert Buist saw Rose du Roi in England in 1831 and noted that it was carefully fenced to keep admirers at a distance. Thomas Rivers believed every garden should grow Crimson Perpetual roses for bouquets in August, September and October on account of beautiful fragrance, rich colour and perfect form.

These roses could be used as a low garden hedge of 3 ft / 90 cm, or in limited space where a splash of crimson is needed. With all Portlands it is imperative to carefully deadhead immediately after flowering, allowing each short-stemmed bud to develop fully and flower over a long season.

Comte de Chambord

Of the first Portlands, Rose du Roi played an important part in the development of Hybrid Perpetuals, and a few later fully-double hybrids were originally classed as such and were included by English and American growers in their long lists of that class. However, as these clearly show Damask characteristics, they are now recognised as Portlands.

Comte de Chambord provides an old-rose form in autumn, and, towards the end of October, its full-petalled lilac-pink flowers deepening towards the centre are outstanding in the large walled rose garden at Castle Howard. Jacques Cartier has a flatter form of the same colour though its small petals are slightly curled. There is a charming white variety, Blanc de Vibert which has a hint of lemon, though this rose is more readily available abroad than in England. Of the darker shades, Arthur de Sansal has small quartered flowers shaded maroon and purple, Delambre's dark pink merges to crimson and, while Marbrée is prettily marbled pale crimson and pink, it has, unlike the others, little scent.

These roses will grace any mixed planting. Their compact display can prove very useful for central border planting with companions of delicate foliage, like gypsophila, artemesia or polemonium. All Portlands, flowering late, need to be carefully thinned of old wood and reshaped in the spring.

Old Blush China

At the turn of the eighteenth century, a revolution in the world of roses was caused by the introduction to the West of four garden varieties from China. When crossed with old summer flowerers, exciting roses with new characteristics of flower, foliage, colour and important long-flowering habit resulted. One of these, named Parsons's Pink China for its grower at Rickmansworth and probably the same as Old Blush we grow today, proved a prolific parent.

John Champneys of South Carolina used it with the old white musk (*R. moschata*) to produce Champneys' Pink Cluster, a repeat-flowering climber. From this, Philippe Noisette of Charleston raised Old Blush Noisette, and sent it to his brother Louis in Paris, who established the new class. On the Isle de Bourbon in the Indian Ocean (now Réunion) it was used for hedging with Autumn Damask, a chance cross resulting in the locally named Rose Edouard and subsequent development of Bourbon roses in France.

Old Blush also produced compact China hybrids like Irene Watts, flat, double, pale pink, and Hermosa, globular, and of deeper shade. The latter was a favourite of George V – he planted thousands at Sandringham in Norfolk. A group of three will make a good show in the average garden, flowering almost incessantly for five months, as does Old Blush itself – an excellent garden rose of 4 x 2 ft / 1.2 m x 60 cm which will attain twice that height on a wall.

Cramoisi Supérieur

As important as Old Blush China in rose history, the China rose named *R. semperflorens*, and Slater's Crimson *Rosa*, contributed a new deep scarlet-crimson and red-tinged foliage to its hybrids and is believed to be responsible for practically all our bright-red long-flowering roses. Unlike Old Blush, its spindly, twiggy growth did not commend it for the garden and it was lost until rediscovered some forty years ago in Bermuda, a regular rose repository for ships trading between East and West.

Of early progeny, Cramoisi Supérieur (1832) received immediate and deservedly long-lasting acclaim for its compact shape of 3 x 2 ft / 90 x 60 cm. It bears small double blooms of deepest crimson, typical small dark, shiny leaves and red prickles. Robert Buist exhorted every American collector to procure one. Twenty years later Thomas Rivers believed there to be no rose more beautiful with "flowers so finely formed … tints so rich". Still later in the century, William Paul rated it among the best for constancy of bloom in massed planting. The climbing variety is as spectacular, but flowers less.

Fabvier, a slightly-shorter hybrid of the same date, has an occasional streak of white on deep scarlet-crimson, semi-double flowers and Louis Philippe (1834), with some petals edged blush white, is more readily available in America than elsewhere at present. These early China hybrids made ideal planting for the garden of 1830–40 when the fashion was for small clumps of brilliant colour.

Rosa chinensis mutabilis

The origin of this single China, not long known in the west, is obscure. The shade of most true China roses darkens with age, as opposed to usual fading; Mutabilis opens dramatically from a pointed flame-orange bud to a loose pale buff-yellow flower, changing next day to copper-pink and on the third to crimson before dropping. A bush in full flush of every stage is a wonderful sight, worthy of a place in every garden and, moreover, it is hardy and disease-free, flowering from May until the first frosts. Purplish stems bear small, pointed leaves of metallic red tints to complement the flowers perfectly on an open bush of up to 8 ft / 2.5 m. It will reach twice that height on a wall, as it does at Kiftsgate Court, in Gloucestershire.

A similar soft buff-yellow was acclaimed in 1824 with the introduction of Parks's Yellow Tea-Scented China to complete the important quartet, following that of Hume's Blush Tea-Scented China in 1809 and both were taken to Prince and Buist in 1828. They evolved from *R. chinensis* x *R. gigantea*, the Wild Tea Rose, to bestow soft pinks and yellows on subsequent Teas and Hybrid Teas – tenderness of Hume's Blush and Parks's Yellow restricts availability today. They have the same form. They open from oval buds to globular flowers which incline gracefully from a thin, red flower stalk and, within 24 hours on a hot summer day, unfold to loose, double blooms of softly-curving large petals amongst young foliage, burnished red.

Désprez à Fleur Jaune

The influence of Parks's Yellow soon became apparent in some early Noisettes, of which Désprez à Fleur Jaune (1835) is one of the most beautiful of this exceptionally fragrant, long-flowering class of climbers. From a union with Blush Noisette resulted a quartered flower with shades of apricot, yellow, pink and buff, which Buist believed was better planted for close viewing than at a distance. It was included in the 1848 list of Ashdown Nurseries, Burlington, New Jersey, with thirteen others, some described as "needing slight protection in winter". In England, it reaches 20 x 10 ft / 6 x 3 m on the wall between the first and second collections at Mottisfont.

William Paul, England's leading rosarian of the nineteenth century, regretted the trend to hybridise Noisettes with tender Tea-Scented Roses and of the forty he listed, only eighteen were hardy varieties, useful for any wall situation or as weeping standards and pillars. These included Aimée Vibert, pure white blooms in large clusters, Céline Forestier, shaded yellow-peach of moderate growth and pale blush Miss Glegg, available in California today.

Tender Lamarque, first of the Tea-Scented Noisettes (1830) has nodding, pale straw-coloured flowers and in England must be grown on a very warm, sheltered wall or under glass. An early account from South Carolina told of an 8-year-old example covering a substantial verandah with flowers from May to December. Its seedling, Cloth of Gold thrives beautifully in temperate New Zealand.

Souvenir de la Malmaison

The rose from the Isle de Bourbon (see p. 32) reached England via Paris by 1825 and was in America three years later. Subsequent Bourbons charmed William Paul with their clear colours, smooth petals, circular outline and beautiful foliage. William Buist believed they would become the most widely cultivated roses north of Virginia and, indeed, for a few decades they were in great demand on both sides of the Atlantic.

Souvenir de la Malmaison was collected as an unnamed variety from that garden by the Grand Duke of Russia and, when back in St. Petersburg, he named it to commemorate his visit. The fully-quartered, fragrant creamy-pink flowers recur from June to October, whereas the climbing variety only flowers twice and the early blooms are usually poorly shaped. This was introduced by Henry Bennett in 1890 and will reach 12 ft / 3.5 m in sun or shade. Sixty years later a charming sport of the original was discovered in Ireland, and was named Souvenir de St. Anne's. This variety inherited recurrent flowering with paler flowers of fewer petals making a substantial bush of 7 ft / 2 m, suitable for the back of a large mixed border, accompanied by blue iris for contrast of colour and foliage shape.

Coupe d'Hebe and Madame Lauriol de Barny, both soft pink, respond well and echo the full blooms of their old summer rose ancestors.

Louise Odier

This Bourbon endorses William Paul's admiration of a circular outline and, when lilac-pink Louise Odier first arrived in England from France in 1855, it was advertised as "most distinctive and should be in every collection". Later, Reine Victoria, of the same shape, had deeper pink, almost translucent petals and Madame Pierre Oger brought to the group a creamed blush which deepens in strong sunlight. Planted as a border trio, slender and upstanding, these Bourbons hold their heads high and do not take up a great deal of space. Their form is emphasised by planting softly rotund companions: artemisia, caryopteris and senecio, with neat *Nepeta nervosa* below.

Other Bourbons suit different situations. Commandant Beaurepaire needs space and no distraction to display its dramatic flowers, which appear mainly at midsummer. The 5 x 5 ft / 1.5 x 1.5 m bush can be grown alone in grass where long stems incline gracefully to present cupped blooms splashed with many shades of pink, crimson and purple. Honorine de Brabant, more delicately striped with purplish tones on pale lilac, grows to 8 ft / 2.5 m and two could be used for an archway or where a moderate climber is needed, although it is not listed as such. The same applies to Madame Isaac Periere, whose voluptuous cerise-magenta blooms have outstanding fragrance and, if grown on the house near a west window, will flood the room on a summer evening.

Général Jacqueminot

Bourbons remained predominant until about 1850 when they were overtaken by roses arising from an amalgamation of Portlands and Bourbons, known as Hybrid Perpetuals, although they were not perpetual but *remontant* – flowering well in the autumn. They were acclaimed world-wide until almost the end of the century for their hardiness and large spectacular flowers, excelling at fiercely-competitive rose shows. Having so many forebears, the blooms of these roses differ widely: cupped, flat, high-centred, quartered, or rosette and colours range from white to deepest crimson, maroon, and purple, with no yellow among them. Their foliage is rather coarse and bushes, upright or lax, are best displayed with a little manipulation.

Among the earliest varieties, deep crimson Général Jacqueminot (1853) proved a universal favourite, acclaimed by nurserymen in Europe, America and the Antipodes. Henderson of New York rated it the most fashionable of all roses or winter flowers. The popularly-known "General Jack" produced Charles Lefèbvre, an upright 4 x 3 ft / 1.2 m x 90 cm rose with larger crimson-maroon flowers, excellent for exhibiting. A lanky semi-double from the latter, Souvenir du Dr. Jamain, is best planted on a west wall, its even darker purplish-crimson flowers burning in full sun. Tall, blue campanulas make good companions for these dusky roses, with pale violas for underplanting.

Baron Girod de l'Ain

Although shaded, rich reds are often considered the best Hybrid Perpetuals, there are rewarding alternatives. Fragrant flowers of Baron Girod de l'Ain are arresting with their deckled white edges on cupped petals, the outer leaves reflexing gracefully. A more gentle variety is found in Vick's Caprice, an American introduction of 1897 which has red buds opening to a soft pink, striped blush, on a compact bush. Of clear pink varieties, both Mrs John Laing and Baroness Rothschild grow upright. They have a good scent, the former being particularly useful for cutting. White – rare in this class now – is well represented by the robust Gloire Lyonnaise, a rose mentioned in the *Proceedings* of the Pennsylvania Horticultural Society of 1905 as being particularly suitable for Philadelphia's climate. An east-facing position in my own garden provides no deterrent to this pristine example.

Early Hybrid Perpetuals were often disciplined on pillars or by pegging down to form low arches of bloom. This method is well demonstrated at Mottisfont where 5 ft / 1.5 m stems are attached to the base of other bushes. For fronting a border, stout metal tent pegs provide firm anchorage for the festoons of rich scarlet-crimson Hugh Dickson and the lighter Ulrich Brunner, both of which respond well to this treatment. It is essential with this technique to cut out old stems from the base and train down brittle shoots gradually to avoid snapping.

Général Schablikine

Concurrently with the Hybrid Perpetuals, another class was being developed from the two Tea-Scented Chinas (see p. 36) many of which had new, soft shades of yellow, peach, pink and copper. These less robust Tea Roses were first kept in conservatories for protection, although some are hardy, for example, brick-red Monsieur Tillier which is excellent for cutting, and Général Schablikine, whose coppery-pink blooms are continuously produced, as can be seen near the entrance to the Mottisfont Rose Garden.

However, those that can be grown in Britain in no way compare with the large bushes I have seen flourishing in California and New Zealand, where buff-yellow Safrano, Perle des Jardins and Solfaterre bloom practically the whole year round. In colder climates it is worthwhile planting these varieties in suitably large containers for summer enjoyment near the house and transferring to a cool greenhouse or other protection. Buist, for example, advised planting in a perforated barrel to protect against the Pennsylvanian winter.

Whether planted on pots or open ground, Teas should not be pruned until late spring on account of possible damage to soft wood. In extreme winter conditions they may be protected with a covering of small evergreen branches. Alliums, which also appreciate the warmest spot in the garden, prove unobtrusive companions for Tea Roses of subtle shades.

Gloire de Dijon

One of the best-loved climbers since its introduction in 1853, Gloire de Dijon resulted from a cross between a Tea Rose and Souvenir de la Malmaison. It was rated highly for symmetry, size, endurance, colour and perfume and dubbed a "good all-rounder" for every garden purpose by Dean Reynolds Hole, an eminent Victorian rosarian. By 1858 it was advertised in Australia as "the finest Tea Rose in cultivation" and offered at more than double the price of all other roses by a Melbourne nursery. In England it became popularly known as Old Glory and was said to adorn practically every porch in the Isle of Wight.

The first-recognised Tea Rose, Adam (1825), of like colour although more tender, is not listed as a climber but will reach some 8 ft / 2.5 m on a sheltered wall. The same situation suits Devoniensis, bred in England (1836) and Sombreuil, both true climbing Teas of moderate height and with pale apricot-tinted centres inside full white blooms. A century ago, the former was listed among the most satisfactory Teas in California, its climate ideal for this class, whereas Hybrid Perpetuals preferred the rigorous eastern United States. Climbing Lady Hillingdon displays soft apricot flowers with a delicious fragrance over an archway at Wisley Gardens. The delicate refinement of Teas is worthy of protection in rose gardens of today.

Perle d'Or

In 1875 a *R. multiflora* hybrid heralded a new class of small polyantha roses, some showing a marked Tea influence, for example, an orange-cream Perle d'Or. Because of its perfectly-scrolled buds and miniature flowers, it was also known as the "Buttonhole Rose" and it makes a slender 4 ft / 1.2 m bush; a group of three backed by delphiniums is admirable for a yellow and blue border planting. Cécile Brunner is half this height, its pale silvery pink flowers of the same form earning it another name, the "Sweetheart Rose" and it looks well when potted for continuous patio display. These charming little roses were immediately appreciated by florists on both sides of the Atlantic.

Confusion sometimes arises between Cécile Brunner and the so-called Bloomfield Abundance (also known as Spray Cécile Brunner) but the distinction lies in the latter's longer calyx lobes. It is also much taller, reaching up to 6 ft / 1.8 m with red stems of open growth and forming a delicate ornamental shrub rose. The climbing form of Cécile Brunner flowers in summer only, but will make a decorative display up to 25 ft / 7.5 m.

In the early part of this century dwarf polyanthas were developed in quantity and these produced surprising colour breaks – the orange-scarlet Gloria Mundi, for example – only to be made redundant by their universally-popular offspring, the floribunda or cluster roses, although they are now making a comeback.

Rosa rugosa alba

At the end of the eighteenth century *rugosas* were brought to Europe from the Far East where they had long been cultivated and used domestically. Another century elapsed, however, before they reached our gardens. This species has large flowers blooming over many months with dark green glossy foliage turning gold, orange-red hips high in vitamin C content and very prickly stems, often put to good use as an impenetrable hedge. White *R. r. alba* is more desirable than *R. r. typica*, as the latter's vivid pink blooms clash with fruit. They are disease resistant, and will tolerate poor soil and harsh weather, which makes them ideal for roadside planting and controlling sand erosion, naturalising on eastern American coasts.

When thoughts turned to wild gardens under the influence of William Robinson in 1883, breeders capitalised on obvious *rugosa* qualities and the list is long today. A selection of four for the average garden might include the rich-crimson-purple Roseraie de l'Hay, soft yellow Agnes (both substantial bushes which grow up to 6 ft / 1.8 m), slightly-smaller creamy-white Schneezwerg which has orange-red hips and, of a more compact form, Fru Dagmar Hastrup, whose pale-pink blooms associate well with crimson hips. They need no support and will provide lasting interest in the garden with their bold, fragrant flowers, lively foliage and conspicuous fruit.

Alberic Barbier

A change of rose fashion occurred at the end of the nineteenth century, Alberic Barbier being among the first of new small-flowered, pliant-stemmed ramblers. These were a welcome contrast to large formal blooms which dominated the previous era and were eminently suitable for decorative gardening. With hybridisation between two vigorous fragrant species from the Far East and new roses of varied colour, a wonderful medley was produced.

Alberic Barbier inherited typical glossy *R. wichuraiana* foliage, its soft yellow-cream loose flowers from Tea Rose Shirley Hibberd continuing well into the autumn. This has always been a favourite, as has the coppery-pink Albertine which came later from the same French breeder. Both inherited lengthy growth, reaching 20 ft / 3.5 m. In contrast *R. multiflora* makes a dense spreading bush of 12 ft / 3.5 m with large trusses of tiny single white flowers. The yellow-cream hybrid Goldfinch will also make an excellent bushy shrub.

Ramblers should have old wood cut out after flowering and new growth should be carefully trained in position for the next year's display. Some Wichuraianas can be allowed to ramble on the ground. This trailing species was originally known in America as the Memorial Rose on account of its wide use in cemeteries. Multifloras tend to flower early so a careful choice will spread the once-flowering ramblers over a maximum period.

Rosa moyesii

Wild roses are indigenous only in the Northern Hemisphere and of the known 140 species, *R. moyesii* is outstanding and probably the most spectacular in terms of flower and fruit. It was discovered by E. H. Wilson in Western Hupeh, China, when collecting for Kew Gardens and the Arnold Arboretum in Boston, and was named by him for a hospitable missionary, the Rev. J. Moyes. Growth is tall (12 ft / 3.5 m), with a slender outline below long branches curving outwards from the top to form an umbrella for shade-loving plants below. The early, deep crimson-red flowers are borne along these high stems from which large flagon-shaped hips dangle in autumn.

China is the most prolific source of beautiful wild roses and some were collected by missionaries; for example, *R. hugonis* by a Father Hugh. This grows to a rounded 7 ft / 2 m bush with ferny foliage and tiny single primrose-yellow flowers that always remain cupped. The hips are small and dark and unspectacular, but this species presents a fresh spring picture.

R. omiensis pteracantha from Western China is an unusual rose. It has only four delicate white petals and enormous flat blood-red prickles randomly placed on bristly stems. This 10 ft / 3 m species should be planted where sunlight from behind will fire them more intensely. They turn dull after the first season and stems must be cut from the base to encourage spectacular new growth.

Index